PREVENTING WORKPLACE THEFT
They're Stealing from You

Lynn Tylczak
Thomas E. Sheets

A FIFTY-MINUTE™ SERIES BOOK

CRISP PUBLICATIONS, INC.
Menlo Park, California

PREVENTING WORKPLACE THEFT
They're Stealing from You

Lynn Tylczak
Thomas E. Sheets

CREDITS
Managing Editor: **Kathleen Barcos**
Editor: **Kay Keppler**
Typesetting: **ExecuStaff**
Cover Design: **Carol Harris**
Artwork: **Ralph Mapson**

Copyright © 1995 by Crisp Publications, Inc.

Printed in the United States of America by Bawden Printing Company.

English language Crisp books are distributed worldwide. Our major international distributors include:

CANADA: Reid Publishing Ltd., Box 69559—109 Thomas St., Oakville, Ontario, Canada L6J 7R4. TEL: (905) 842-4428, FAX: (905) 842-9327

Raincoast Books Distribution Ltd., 112 East 3rd Avenue, Vancouver, British Columbia, Canada V5T 1C8. TEL: (604) 873-6581, FAX: (604) 874-2711

AUSTRALIA: Career Builders, P.O. Box 1051, Springwood, Brisbane, Queensland, Australia 4127. TEL: 841-1061, FAX: 841-1580

NEW ZEALAND: Career Builders, P.O. Box 571, Manurewa, Auckland, New Zealand. TEL: 266-5276, FAX: 266-4152

JAPAN: Phoenix Associates Co., Mizuho Bldg. 2-12-2, Kami Osaki, Shinagawa-Ku, Tokyo 141, Japan. TEL: 3-443-7231, FAX: 3-443-7640

Selected Crisp titles are also available in other languages. Contact International Rights Manager Suzanne Kelly at (415) 323-6100 for more information.

Library of Congress Catalog Card Number 94-72275
Tylczak, Lynn and Thomas E. Sheets
Preventing Workplace Theft
ISBN 1-56052-272-0

This book is printed on recyclable paper with soy ink.

ABOUT THIS BOOK

Preventing Workplace Theft is not like most books. It has a unique "self-study" format that encourages a reader to become personally involved. Designed to be "read with a pencil," the book offers an abundance of exercises, activities, assessments and cases that invite participation.

This book is the only employee-theft book written *for* employees. It graphically demonstrates why employee theft is as much a problem for employees as it is for managers. It helps employees decide not to steal—and shows them how to turn the tables on a peer that does.

Preventing Workplace Theft can be used effectively in a number of ways. Here are some possibilities:

—**Individual Study**. Because the book is self-instructional, all that is needed is a quiet place, some time and a pencil. By completing the activities and exercises, a reader should not only receive valuable feedback, but also take practical steps in creating an honest and safe workplace for all.

—**Workshops and Seminars.** This book is ideal for reading prior to a workshop or seminar. With the basics in hand, the quality of participation will improve. More time can be spent in concept extensions and applications during the program. The book is also effective when a trainer distributes it at the beginning of a session and leads participants through the contents.

—**Remote Location Training**. Copies can be sent to those not able to attend "home office" training sessions.

There are other possibilities that depend on the objectives, program or ideas of the user. One thing is certain: even after it has been read, this book will serve as excellent reference material that can be easily reviewed.

ABOUT THE AUTHORS

Lynn Tylczak is a consultant, author and professional speaker who has written 15 books, including *Attacking Absenteeism, Downsizing Without Disaster* and *Reduce Your Property Tax,* published by Crisp. She has also written more than 150 articles on business issues such as credits and collections, taxes, and employee productivity.

Lynn has appeared on CNN, FNN, and "The Today Show." She has been profiled by the *New York Times, Woman's Day* and *The Saturday Evening Post.*

Thomas Sheets is director of corporate security for Consolidated Freightways, Inc. and is a certified fraud examiner.

He has previously served more than six years as director of industrial relations and security for a major Florida corporation, and ten years as an investigator in the Orange County, Florida, prosecutor's office.

Thomas has chaired the International Association of Cargo Security Professionals, and is a member of the American Society of Industrial Security Standing Committee on Transportation, the International Association of Chiefs of Police, and the U.S. Department of State Overseas Advisory Council.

Thomas received his bachelor's and master's degrees in Criminal Justice from Rollins College, Florida, and is a graduate of the FBI National Academy.

CONTENTS

INTRODUCTION

By any other name this rose would still smell to high heaven. Call it what you will.

- Employee pilferage

- "Shrinkage" or "shortages"

- The case of the Disappearing Inc.

- Missing merchandise

- Unintended employee perks

- Helping (themselves) hands

- A little look-the-other-way larceny

What's in a name? Nothing. These names are nothing more than the euphemisms we use to describe something most people would rather not address, namely:

- Theft

- Stealing

- Embezzlement

- Criminal behavior

Euphemisms can not mask—nor mitigate—an ugly problem. Employee theft is wrong. Stealing is a criminal act that can have repercussions beyond a prison term. Thieves can wreck their work records when they develop police records and hurt their family, employer and coworkers as well.

It's your duty both as a valued employee and as a concerned citizen to help stop the stealing. The tips in this book will show you how. Remember: The best way to take a bite out of crime is to have honest employees like you sink their teeth into the problem.

INTRODUCTION (continued)

To quote a former thief (now serving a prison term), "The worst thing about getting caught was the look on my kids' faces when they found out I was going to jail. That, and the fact that I don't think I can ever look my parents in the face again."

"Still, I can't blame anybody but myself. When I chose to steal I accepted the risks of getting caught. I was an idiot."

P A R T

I

Employee Theft:
The Invisible Problem

EMPLOYEE THEFT AWARENESS EXERCISE #1

How much do you really know about the prevalence of theft by employees in the workplace? Do you know its financial and psychological impact, or who really are the injured parties? Answer the following true or false questions, then check your answers with those at the bottom of the page.

T/F

____ 1. More than two-thirds of all retail employees steal more than once a year.

____ 2. Theft of very small, inexpensive items is expected and has little or no effect on a company's bottom-line profits.

____ 3. The financial loss to employers from employees who steal is very minor compared to theft from outsiders.

____ 4. Most employees who steal feel that they are justified in their actions.

____ 5. Employees often steal in groups rather than by themselves.

____ 6. Employees who steal only hurt themselves.

____ 7. A few employees who steal can cause management to penalize all employees.

____ 8. A typical attitude of an employee who steals is that it is no big deal.

____ 9. Adults with families to support are those most likely to begin to steal from their employers.

____ 10. For every dollar an employer loses to shoplifting, bad checks and robberies, $3 is lost to employee theft.

Answers: 1. True; 2. False; 3. False; 4. True; 5. True; 6. False; 7. True; 8. True; 9. False; 10. False ($15 is lost)

If you missed any of the answers, don't be too surprised. Few people know the true impact of workplace theft. Read on to find out more about this growing problem.

YES, BUT . . .

You are probably thinking, "Sure, I'd help stop employee theft, but it just isn't a problem in my company." You had better think again.

Insider stealing does not have to be highly visible to have an effect on a business and its employees. Employee theft is like the common cold: It is everywhere, it affects everyone, it makes us all miserable and it is hard to get rid of. Consider this.

► For every $1 a retailer loses because of shoplifting, fraud, bad checks, burglaries and robberies, $15 are lost to employee theft.

   In short, according to the statistics, a retail employer has more to fear from his employees than he has to fear from other "common criminals." And he pays them for their pilfering.

► Inventory shortages (e.g., inventory that is no longer in stock but was not legitimately sold) at convenience stores is up to about 2% and growing rapidly. Unfortunately, when thefts are growing, profits aren't.

► About 3% of dishonest retail employees steal daily, 7.6% steal every week, 19.7% steal between four and twelve times a year, and 69.7% steal once or twice a year.

   Food for thought: Consistent and continuing thefts can add up. An employee doesn't need to steal large or expensive items to have a significant effect on the company's bottom line.

   Assume that you are a supermarket employee. A coworker steals a large bottle of soda and deli sandwich every day. The items have a combined retail value of $4. *If this employee works at the store for a full year (approximately 200 days) and takes the same items every day, he will steal $800 worth of merchandise annually.*[1] That's an $800 "job benefit" *you* did not receive.

► If an employee in a convenience store steals just $5,000 worth of merchandise, the store must increase sales by $166,666.66 to recoup that loss because the net profit margin is 3% on merchandise.

▶ In the United States alone, employees stole money, merchandise and miscellaneous materials worth almost $120 billion in 1988, a figure that has been increasing at a rate of about 15% a year. To put that figure in perspective, $120 billion is ten times the annual amount lost to street crime.

▶ The high cost of living is just one cost associated with high employee crime rates. The cost of employee pilfering is passed on to consumers, adding (on average) about 15% to product prices.

Compare *that* 15% figure to today's inflation rate and you'll see why curbing employee crime is a consumer concern. When an employee steals, consumers end up paying the bills.

▶ According to a survey conducted by Reid Psychological Systems, about 26% of manufacturing employees and 42% of retail employees admit to on-site stealing.

▶ Four cents out of every food service dollar is lost to employee theft, costing restaurants almost $9 billion in annual revenues.

▶ In the average business, if an employee steals $100 (in cash or merchandise) the other employees must sell twenty-three items at $100 each just to break even. That means more work for people like *you* and more money for people like *them*.

Note: In truth, those 23 sales of $100 ($2300 total) don't make up for the initial $100 loss. Why? The profit embedded in that $2300— approximately $100— is used to cover the missing $100. In that sense, the $100 in profits is lost, too. The company has to throw good money after bad employee behavior.

▶ *The average employee thief[2] steals seven times as much as the average shoplifter—$1,350 vs. $196.* In short, pilfering employees not only steal more often, they steal more money or merchandise.

▶ Approximately 50%-70% of a retail company's losses are due to employee theft.

▶ If your employer goes under and you lose your job, a major "failure factor" could be employee theft. It's clear that when a colleague buys into a life of crime he is selling his coworkers short.

YES, BUT . . . (continued)

Turning in a pilfering peer is more than just the right thing to do. It's also the smart thing to do. It just may help you save your employer—and your own job.

► Companies spend almost $40 billion a year on commercial security.

Clearly, crime costs. It costs you as an employee, and it costs you as a consumer. What's worse, employee theft can cost you your future; it can cost you your job. You can't thrive if your employer doesn't survive.

Observations

1. Every time an employee gets a "$4 thrill" he or she runs the risk of being caught and losing a job, livelihood, reputation, references and maybe even freedom. Talk about selling yourself short.

2. Chances are, when an employee is "caught in the act" of stealing it isn't the first time he or she has staged a crime. The Loss Prevention Manager for a large chain of West Florida grocery stores caught a cashier pocketing $1.29 of the store's money. The cashier eventually admitted having stolen $6000 in the prior two-and-one-half months.

REALITY CHECKS

You've seen the numbers, now let's put a face on the picture of employee theft. When you read the following essays* note those items in italics. What do they tell you about the attitudes of the people involved?

Reality Check #1

The Food Filcher

When I first started working at the store, I was busy trying to learn the ropes and please my employers. *I didn't engage in stealing until I began working stock a few weeks later.*[3] I usually worked evenings and nights, and I quickly got to know my coworkers because the shift was small. One guy and I had a mutual friend, so we hit it off. Since he had worked at the store for a few years, *he showed me all the ins and outs of stealing.*[4] I'll call him "M."

M introduced me to getting *free* cans of Coke simply by taking them off the shelf and pouring them into paper cups. This practice *didn't seem bad* because the cost was only about 30 cents. Pretty soon I was taking candy and potato chips to eat along with *my* soda. *I figured the company would never miss them, and the total cost wasn't high. Also, I was just one of many who did the same thing.*[5]

As time went by, I stole more. Eventually, M and I were drinking eight-ounce bottles of beer in the walk-in freezers and taking *real* food—ready-made deli sandwiches, doughnuts, Poptarts and pies. Within a month and a half of starting work, I got to know the deli workers, and they gave me chicken and desserts. We more or less *traded* goods; I'd get them sodas, and they'd give me chicken and biscuits. Several of us would take chicken and biscuits anyway, if no one was around.

After about two and a half months, I was trained as a cashier. Several nights a week, I switched from stock and worked a cash register. When a friend came in to buy a pack of cigarettes—at the time they were 90 cents a pack—he would hand me a dollar bill and I would hit the "no sale" button and give my friend four quarters. Sometimes if friends came to my register with a cart of groceries, I would ring up some items and slide others by. *Nobody could have noticed unless they were watching for it, in which case I wouldn't have done it.*

---

*Reprinted with permission by the author, Leonard E. Dobrin, Associate Professor, Old Dominion University, Norfolk, VA; and the consent of *Security Management* magazine.

REALITY CHECKS (continued)

One night, a group of my friends who were going on a trip to the mountains came into the store to stock up on food. I told them to leave their cart by the dairy section and I would mark down the prices on their items with my price gun while they continued looking for things to buy. For example, I marked a $5 can of peanuts down to 99 cents. There were other items that were not so expensive, but I marked them down as well.

When my friends went to the cash register, I helped bag the groceries. The cashier, realizing they were my friends, began sliding items through without ringing them up. He also let them walk out with three cases of Coke. They probably got $80 worth of groceries for around $40.

Although we, as employees, never discussed our activities, we would do the same for each other's friends. I was never caught, nor was I ever worried about getting caught. In fact, I do not know of any employee who got caught[6] stealing from the store.

Observations

3. Employee thefts may begin as soon as an opportunity presents itself.

4. Employee thefts are often a collaborative crime.

5. Thieves usually try to justify their actions.

6. They were caught but the employees who "caught" them never turned them in. These second employees essentially played the role of "crooked cops."

Reality Check #2
The Stealing Stockperson

My job was to unload boxes from the trucks, open them and stock the shelves. Then I crushed the boxes in a hydraulic crusher, much like a trash compactor.

When the compactor was full, I'd push a button and the front wall would push the contents against the back wall to compact it. When the crusher was full of compacted trash, the back wall would automatically lift and the trash would be pushed out into a large receptacle. All of the employees were given keys to this receptacle in case a box or other item was too big to put into the compactor.

While working the crusher one day, I noticed it had a six- to eight-inch hole rusted out of the back wall. *I thought how easy it would be to steal something by waiting until the outside receptacle was empty and sliding things through the rusted hole using the hydraulic wall.*[7]

At the first opportunity, I tried out my theory. I didn't include any of my friends, because I didn't know if it would work. I pretended to be crushing boxes one day when I dropped in a six-pack of beer. I pushed the button to start the hydraulic arm. I found the right spot to place the beer so it would push through the rusted hole. I later told the rest of the group of my discovery. We decided it would work well, because managers rarely came into the back room. And even if they did, *they wouldn't suspect*[8] that items were being stolen through the trash compactor.

One Friday night, some friends had planned a big party. T, M, C and I were working that night. We told our friends to drive up to the rear trash receptacle around 10:00 p.m. Earlier in the day, we had given them a key to open the back of the trash receptacle.

At about 9:30 p.m., T and M started casually bringing six packs of beer to the compactor in boxes. We took turns dropping beer in the compactor a six-pack at a time and, using the hydraulic wall, pushing the beer through the hole and out the back. We dumped about five cases of beer that night, and our friends used the key to retrieve it from the receptacle. We were the "beer connection" for many months.

Observations

7. Employee creativity is focused not on getting the trash compactor fixed but on stealing.

8. This employee not only took beer, he took advantage of the trust and respect his employer had for him.

REALITY CHECKS (continued)

Reality Check #3

The No-Account Accountant

I was really excited when I first got the job at our accounting firm. It was a big step up for me; I had paid my way through college working at fast food restaurants and boring campus jobs. Goodbye, minimum wage!

I guess the excitement just faded after a while. I wasn't that excited by the accounting. The work was boring, repetitive and exacting. I suppose it also bugged me that I was always working with money that wasn't mine.

It didn't seem fair that I got such a low salary (after investing four years in college!) and such a low-end accounting job. The bosses made all of the accounting decisions. Basically, I was a glorified bookkeeper. Worse, while they continuously made both managerial and accounting mistakes, I was expected to have everything balance to the penny. What a pain!

Looking back, I must have resented my bosses. I knew I was at least as smart as they were. I was aware, for example, that they knew less about how their own business ran than I did. After getting chewed out by my immediate superior one day for a "missing penny," I decided to prove it.

I went to the post office and rented a box. I used my personal computer at home to design a convincing looking logo (I used a very generic company name) and some billing statements that showed my post office box as the billing address. I wrote up a bill for our office—I kept the amount due very small the first time, because I didn't want the bill to attract attention—and mailed it in.

I paid my own "bill" right along with the other accounts payable on the 10th of the month. My boss signed the check along with about fifty others (I could write the checks but, as a standard anti-theft deterent, I couldn't sign them) and never noticed a thing. I mailed the check to myself along with all of the others. Two days later I went to the post office box and picked up my $25 check.

It was easy and I got a real kick out of it. The bosses had put me in charge of mundane work so they could keep track of what I was doing. Ha! *Actually, it didn't seem like stealing*. It felt more like I was beating them at a game. Of course, the money did help.

I figure that the six years I worked there I probably stole about $15,000. They never caught me, either.

Reality Check #4

The Hypocrite In Housewares

While I was in *high school,*[9] I worked as a salesperson in the housewares department of a large, medium-to-high-priced department store. About eight months after I began working, I stole for the first time.

At closing, we were required to add up and record all cash in the register. I wanted to go out with some friends that night, and I didn't have any money with me. So, *without even thinking about*[10] what I was doing, I put a $20 bill in my pocket and added up the remaining cash.

What I had done didn't really dawn on me until I was with my friends. I thought, "That was really stupid. *What if someone saw me?*"[11] Yet, no one had.

Three weeks later, two friends came to see me at work about 10 minutes before closing time. They wanted to go out that night, but this time they didn't have any money. I walked over to the register and took $20 out and quickly put it in my friend's pocket. This time I didn't even worry about being caught. "It's so easy," I thought. I was sure many other employees did the same thing when they closed their registers.

I continued to justify my actions to myself whenever I did it again, And I also thought, "This store won't miss $20 anyway." I never did get caught taking any money.

Observations

9. Employees with fewer than two years on the job are responsible for two-thirds of the thefts. Those 16 to 22 years old commit 67% of the crimes.

10. "Without even thinking" is a justification, not an explanation.

11. Note that for this employee, the issue wasn't stealing. The issue was getting caught.

REALITY CHECKS (continued)

Reality Check #5

The Stereo Stealer

I began working at a discount stereo chain. After about two months, I was familiar with the store procedures and was *given more hours with a slight raise in pay.*[12]

More hours meant I stayed later in the evening. *Friends who worked in other stores had told how they had taken various items.* Understanding store operations and hearing the stories, I realized how easy it would be to steal from the store and get away with it.

The opportunity to steal came several times, but I shied away from it, feeling I would be caught. I kept wondering whether it would be worth it. If I got caught, I knew I would be fired. The thought of possibly facing criminal charges frightened me. I knew my parents would be very disappointed and would lose trust in me, which was the last thing I wanted.

One night near the end of my shift, the manager told me to clean up the stockroom. I was the only person in the stockroom. No other employees were in sight. I grabbed a car radio and put it in the trash bag I had been filling. Before anyone could see, I took the trash bag out the back door and placed it near the dumpster. What I had done looked legitimate; after all, I was just taking the trash outside. I then went back to my section of the store as if nothing had happened.

When the store closed, I went to a friend's house. I waited until I knew no one would be around the store, inside or out, before I went back to claim what I had hidden. Sure enough, *my* trash bag was still out back with *my* radio inside. I removed the radio as quickly as possible, thinking that someone might walk up, and got out of the area.

For the next couple of days at work, I was nervous. I was afraid the boss would call me into the office and tell me someone had seen me taking the radio. If anyone had asked me about stealing, *I would have denied it.*[13] I kept in touch with other employees, though, in case they heard anything.

I never told anyone in the store about stealing the radio, because you never know who might be an informer. Other employees mentioned how they put cassette tapes and other small items in their pockets. Once in a while my friends would give me a few dollars if I'd steal things for them. It was an opportunity to make a little extra money; after all, *I wasn't getting paid enough!*

Most of the employees, particularly the younger ones, stole from the store. It was just too easy to steal without getting caught.

Observations

12. Many thieves see business as a give-and-take situation. The more trust and responsibility they are given, the more they can take. Their actions generate an atmosphere of distrust, which can lead to an environment so restrictive that it is hard for honest employees to work productively.

13. Thieves tend to assuage their consciences by denying responsibility for their actions, denying that they hurt anyone (the company or customers), blaming their employers or claiming loftier goals. You can respond to a theft by asking, if customers have to pay to eat the food, shouldn't you? Would you do this out in the open where the company owner would have a chance to see you? If an employee says that the company makes so much money, it will never miss a few bucks, remind this person how small the profit margin is. If an employee says, "I'd never steal from a person, just the company," remind this person that the employer isn't the only victim. Coworkers and family members also stand to lose.

Petty thieves may also say that they wouldn't steal if they were paid a decent salary, but their perceived need may not be the only motivating factor.

REALITY CHECKS (continued)

Reality Check #6

The Restaurant Robber

My first job at the restaurant was as a dishwasher, then I moved to prep cook. Prep cooks prepared salads, cut and weighted steaks, cut up vegetables and did many other tedious jobs. After about a week of being a prep cook, I started working the front.

My job was to take orders from the waitresses and, if it was a dinner order, put salads on the counter for them to serve. When the salads were taken, I made the sandwiches on the order and gave the ticket to the cook so he could prepare the main courses.

Two walk-in units were outside, a freezer and a refrigerator, that were enclosed by a locked, 10-foot chain link fence.

The prep cooks were responsible for loading and rotating stock when deliveries came in. When out in the walk-ins, one of them frequently would reach into a box, grab a piece of cake and wash it down with a beer. The manager would question people about half-empty beer bottles found outside, but he didn't get very upset. He got really ticked off, though, when he found a half-empty $80 bottle of wine.

As a result, the guys who drank the wine changed their tactics. After they drank wine, they would drop the bottle on the floor, sweep up the glass and put it in the trash. If the manager complained about missing wine, the culprit would say the bottle fell off the shelf and broke.

About 20 employees had access to the walk-ins, and at least 15 of them engaged in this petty thievery. No one ever tried to hide the fact that they consumed goods out of the walk-ins.

About five employees, including me, would put a case of beer or a couple of five-pound boxes of shrimp on top of one of the walk-ins. At the end of the work day, we went outside, climbed the fence and retrieved the merchandise. The manager suspected that this happened, but he only suspected one person, not the rest of us. That one person was fired.

Reality Check #7

Blueprint For A Perfect Crime

I worked as a clerk at an engineering firm. I got a decent salary, but that was only because the managers were so unpleasant to us employees that they couldn't keep workers any other way.

I wanted to get back at them for treating me (and my peers) so badly. I couldn't quit—none of us could—because we needed the money. So I decided to get something back in return for all that I had to put up with.

We always had contractors coming in to get blueprints made on our machine. We charged $2 a sheet—it was petty cash, nothing more. Because the amounts were so small most of the contractors paid us in cash. We usually put the money in our petty cash drawer and used it to buy coffee and other supplies. Occasionally we would supplement this money with a check drawn to petty cash.

We knew the engineers never kept track of petty cash or other accounting things, so we simply started keeping the blueprint money. It never amounted to much, maybe $20-30 a week. The managers never missed it.

SUMMARY

If these true confessions bothered you, great. They should. They were written by people who were both on the wrong side of the law and on the wrong side of what's right.

Now that you're aware of the pilfering problem, the next step is to discover how the problem affects *you*.

Checklist

1. What were the common elements of each "Reality Check"?

_____

_____

_____

2. If you were a coworker of any of these thieves, how could you be affected by their illegal actions?

_____

_____

_____

3. How could these thefts have been prevented?

_____

_____

_____

4. Would you be willing to turn them in?

_____

_____

_____

5. What responsibilities does an employee have who spots a coworker engaged in theft from the workplace?

_____

_____

_____

P A R T

II

Why Should *You* Care?

EMPLOYEE THEFT AWARENESS EXERCISE #2

How much do you really know about the impact to you if one of your coworkers steals from the company? Answer the following fill-in-the-blank questions, then check your answers with those at the bottom of the page.

1. Dishonest employees steal from you in terms of _____ available for bonuses, benefits, and raises.

2. If an employer does not know who is stealing from the company, the boss is likely to blame _____ .

3. Employee theft can have _____ on the sales commissions other employees might earn.

4. Allowing a co-worker to _____ can cost you a pleasant working environment.

5. Employee theft is the concern of management, stockholders, customers, and _____ .

Answers: 1. money; 2. everyone; 3. a significant effect; 4. steal; 5. you

If you missed any of the answers, read on. Most people think that if they personally are not stealing, then there is no real consequence or effect for them as employees. If you are one of these people, think again!

WHY YOU *SHOULD* CARE

Many businesses have a pilferage problem. Whose problem is it? Is it the problem of:

► Top management?

► Middle management?

► The stockholders?

► The customers?

► Or honest employees, that is, you?

Obviously employee theft is top management's problem. Top management is responsible for the overall performance of a business. If employee theft hurts overall profits, it undercuts the business.

Employee theft is also a middle management problem. Overall performance is the sum performance of many departments. If a divisions' profits slip because its employees steal, those managers are in trouble. They may see their careers cut short.

Stockholders also have a stake in the stealing. A business's value is a function of its performance. High profits generate a high (and increasing) stock value; low profits depress a company's net worth. If a company loses merchandise and money to its employees to the extent that profits fall, stockholders will be shortchanged.

Employee pilferage is a 15% surcharge that no customer wants to pay. In addition, when merchandise is missing, the odds are decreased that a customer will be able to buy what he wants when he wants it.

But the biggest losers of all may be the honest employees. In other words, people like you.

The following pages will open your eyes and, perhaps, cause you to see employee theft in different light.

THEIR GAIN IS YOUR LOSS

Dishonest employees don't just take money out of your employer's pocket. They take it our of *yours* as well. Here's how.

A business only makes so much money. Money that is lost to employee theft is not available for:

► Raises

► Bonuses

► Profit sharing

► Retirement contributions

► Better health care benefits

► Additional vacation or sick leave

► On-site child care

► Improved working conditions

► Employee education, training or growth

► Business growth

A thief's gain is purchased at the cost of your own. That's a terrible trade-off. However, in some companies, money not lost to employee theft is used to pay those employees who report internal theft. Many companies reward helpful and honest employees with trips, cash or gift certificates (most often worth between $50 and $500) or store merchandise. Under information incentive programs, everyone wins but the thief. And isn't that the way it should be? Responsible employees keep the welfare and success of the business establishment in mind at all times and recognize that their own success is tied to that of the business.

TARNISHED TRUST

When your colleagues steal money and merchandise from the business, they also take something intangible away from your employee-employer relationship. The company spirit changes from "all for one and one for all" to "all for one and that one is me."

Since the bosses don't know whom to trust, they don't trust anyone. As a result, employees like you are penalized by attitudes like these.

- "Why should we give the employees a 20 cent an hour raise? They're already stealing 30! If we give them an inch, they'll take a mile!"

- "We can't afford to run our employee hours/breaks/discounts on the honor system. The employees don't have any honor. Look at the shortages."

- "We'll have to treat our employees with suspicion rather than respect. So from now on, remember we aren't just businesspeople. We're babysitters."

It's sad but true: Managers need to play it safe. If statistics document internal theft and the managers don't know who's doing the stealing, they have little choice. They have to treat all of their employees like petty criminals rather than colleagues.

THE "UN"-FAIRNESS FACTOR

It's not fair, but you can be fairly sure that when employees steal, you will pay the penalty for someone else's pilfering. Sometimes the price you pay is swift and sure. For example, if you work in a unit with a high theft rate your department manager will probably treat the entire staff—even you—with distrust. You might even lose a promotional opportunity because of your unit's bad reputation. That's not fair. That's just life.

Here's something else: You may be blamed for somebody else's stealing. Thieves have a lot to lose (their jobs, for example) and that's why they may hedge their bets by setting up coworkers. Don't be surprised if you find stolen money or merchandise in your locker or car. That way you could end up taking the fall for someone else's crime.

Suppose you work for "X" dollars an hour, while the new employee next to you does exactly the same thing and earns $2X" dollars an hour. If you saw this happening, you'd complain to the boss.

The problem is, the boss didn't create this discrepancy. That's because the "X"tra cash your colleague gets doesn't come in a paycheck. It comes under the table.[14]

Observation

14. An employee who steals a "mere" $1.50 an hour has given him- or herself an annual $3,000 a year raise—tax free!

When honest employees ignore internal theft, they can get caught in the crossfire.

24

NO GAIN STRESS AND STRAIN

A business is like a fine handknit sweater. When a dishonest employee pulls a string of thefts, a business can start to unravel.

Here's one example. Assume that Gregory has been stealing merchandise off the shipping dock. He has created a great deal of stress and heartache for:

▶ *Rhea, who credits returns to customer accounts.*

Last week, Mr. Ray claimed that he returned a shipment to the company, but his account was never credited. Rhea has no record of the return; she can't, since Gregory stole the package before it could be processed. It's a case of Mr. Ray's word against her return record.

▶ *Addie, who handles the company's newspaper advertising.*

Addie had intended to feature Brand X in this week's advertising promotion, but because the product hasn't arrived yet, she's frantically looking for another feature. What are her choices? She could hope that the product arrives in time or she could choose a second item. (This brings up another batch of problems: Would she have enough stock of the second product to cover the ad? Does the second product return enough profit to absorb a significant price reduction? Will the second product be as desirable to consumers as the first?) Addie doesn't know the shipment is in Gregory's garage.

▶ *Walter, the hard-hitting salesman.*

Walter should have made big bucks last weekend, but since only half of the sales merchandise came in, half of his potential customers went out empty-handed. Some even went out angry, because they had made an effort to come in only to find the merchandise they wanted wasn't in stock.

The Walters of the world can't sell what they don't have. They can't make money if they can't make sales. Gregory isn't just fooling with the corporate profits, he's fouling up Walter's livelihood.

► *John, who processes the payables.*

John isn't willing to pay for merchandise the company hasn't received, yet several suppliers claimed that their shipments arrived at the company's loading dock. Their independent carrier has delivery signatures to prove it.

John finds himself having to pay for goods sight unseen (and site unknown). He's frustrated. He thinks you should get what you pay for, rather than pay for what you don't or won't get.

An employee who steals creates chaos. And guess who gets to pick up the pieces? People like you! That's why part of your job is making it hard for pilferers to profit.

SULLIED SURROUNDINGS

Have you ever seen a maximum security prison? It's not a pretty sight. Here's what you'd see:

- Lots of guards watching the prisoners' every move

- Security cameras

- Strip searches

- Limited access

- A siege mentality

Have you ever seen a business with a high loss or shortage rate? Here's what you'd see:

- Lots of security guards watching the employees' every move.

- Security cameras

- Personal searches

- Limited access

- A siege mentality

Prisons and businesses plagued by theft have strong parallels. If you want to work in a prison, become a corrections officer. If you don't, help the company prevent pilferage. Don't let pilferers pollute your work environment.

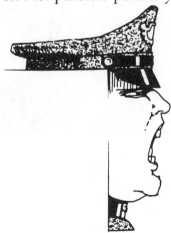

SUMMARY

If your company has a problem with pilferage, you both have a problem. Serious shortages can cost you (and your employer) money, professional and personal opportunities, stress and a pleasant working atmosphere. In short, you don't have to be a thief to be personally—and profoundly—affected by employee theft.

However, it's not enough to recognize that the problem exists. You need to help stop employee theft before employee theft puts a stop to your own success.

Checklist

1. Do you know of a situation similar to those described in this section?

   _____

   _____

   _____

2. How would you react if your job and success was affected by this type of thievery?

   _____

   _____

   _____

3. Are any of the previous situations jeopardizing either your job or the company's financial health?

   _____

   _____

   _____

P A R T

III

What to Look For:
The Seven Signs

EMPLOYEE THEFT AWARENESS EXERCISE #3

Do you know what activities or signs to watch for to tell whether or not a coworker is stealing? Some signs are clear and others are subtle. Answer the following true or false questions, then check your answers with those at the bottom of the page.

T/F

____ 1. Dishonest employees usually fall into a typical profile and their appearance is often the give-away.

____ 2. Coworkers with addictions to drugs or gambling are at high risk of becoming thieves.

____ 3. An employee who insists that someone else process their transactions may be hiding thefts.

____ 4. Employees who ask lots of questions about things not necessary to performing their immediate job might be sizing up ways to steal from the company.

____ 5. Sympathy for a coworker's difficulties is often a good reason not to report them.

____ 6. You should watch more carefully coworkers who always pay cash for expensive items.

____ 7. Coworkers who form tight groups are usually above suspicion because they worry about what the others might think or say.

____ 8. Coworkers who travel a lot for non-work-related reasons are usually above suspicion because they are not around as much and do not have as much opportunity to steal.

____ 9. Gung-ho employees who put in lots of overtime, coming in extra early and staying very late, are usually above suspicion because they are mainly concerned with getting ahead.

____ 10. It is common for employees who steal to pass up promotions.

Answers: 1. False; 2. True; 3. True; 4. True; 5. False; 6. True; 7. False; 8. False; 9. False; 10. True

If you missed any of the answers, read on. These signs may or may not indicate a problem, however the signs are typical and can be cause to be more alert to a coworker's actions.

WHAT TO LOOK FOR

Once upon a time there was a large corporation, the XYZ Corporation, which manufactured Extremely Valuable Items. All of XYZ's products were small, desirable and difficult to track. As a result, employee theft was more than a mere concern—it was a near catastrophe.

The two guards who covered the west gate were sure that they had at least one on-site thief. Every day, just before lunch, Otto—one of the plant's lowest-paid people—would take a wheelbarrow full of garbage to the dumpster outside the plant. Just what it was about Otto that made the guards suspicious, they couldn't say. But because they had their suspicions—and they had a job to do—they never gave him a chance to steal.

Five times a week the guards would rummage through Otto's wheelbarrow, looking for hidden treasures. They searched Otto as well, but they never found any stolen goods. So five times a week, they would let him pass.

The plant closed. Soon after, one of the west gate guards ran into Otto. He was driving a new sports car and wearing expensive new clothes and jewelry. Quite a feat for a man who never made more than $6 an hour.

The former guard approached Otto. "We knew it," the guard cried triumphantly. "We knew you were stealing, even though we were never able to catch you. Well, it's too late to do anything about it now. But please satisfy my curiosity and tell me: how did you do it?"

"It was easy," grinned Otto. "You never caught me because I was stealing wheelbarrows."

The moral of the story is this: If you want to see employee theft you have to know what you're looking for. Evidence isn't always as obvious as it might be, and sometimes behavior that appears to be criminal is nothing more than eccentric.

This chapter will describe some employee theft warning signs. They should alert you to the fact that something *may* be wrong (or someone may be doing wrong). A warning sign is not the same thing as a guarantee. An employee may engage in suspicious behavior without engaging in criminal behavior.

SIGN #1: The Pilferer's Profile

Distinguishing Characteristics Profile

The following distinguishing traits might help you separate your peers from illegal profiteers. Put a checkmark by the features that an employee who steals is most likely possesses.

☐ Part-timer	☐ Full-timer
☐ Short-timer	☐ Long-timer
☐ White collar	☐ Blue collar
☐ Ambitious	☐ Uncertain
☐ Industrious	☐ Indifferent
☐ Teenagers	☐ Pre-retirees
☐ 20- to 30-year-olds	☐ 40- to 50-year-olds
☐ Blonde	☐ Red head
☐ Brunette	☐ Bald
☐ Small	☐ Large
☐ Loud	☐ Quiet

The correct answers, of course, are all of these—and none of these. The point is that one should never pre-judge another person's honesty. Theft is a moral defect, and not associated with any physical or mental traits. Do not try to "spot a thief a mile away." Get close enough to gather and examine specific behavioral evidence. Never use surface criteria to judge a person's honesty. You need evidence, not appearances, to accuse and convict someone of theft. Most employees are honest, and they are all innocent until proven guilty.

SIGN #2: Dollars And Sense Deviations

Money or the lack of it is the major reason that most people steal. As a result, how an employee spends money can indicate if the employee steals it.

The following warning signs often suggest that an employee is stealing at work. Watch for:

► Employees who appear to live beyond their means. Remember, however, that a lavish lifestyle could be supported by inherited wealth or other means.

► Employees who have an unusual—often critical—need for lots of money. Such needs could include divorces (including legal fees, child support and alimony payments), the support of aged parents, high tuition fees or a critically ill dependent.

You probably feel sorry for peers with these problems. You should. Sympathy for those in trouble is human and humane-nature.

Sympathy does not require you to compromise your own moral values or your duty to your employer. Stealing is wrong. No ifs, ands, or buts.

► Employees who are victims of addiction, including gambling, alcohol and other drugs. These employees may steal to support their habit.

An employee's addiction can cost more than mere money. Addicts are often less productive than other employees and more responsible for workplace accidents and violence.

► Employees who pay for big, expensive items in cash.

Most people cannot afford to pay cash for expensive items. They need to plan, to save, and often, use credit. If someone can *always* pay for big-ticket items with cash, it could be because the money was obtained illegally.

SIGN #3: Working Alone

People who steal from their employers know that it's wrong. That's why thieves often hide—rather than confide—their activities. Pilfering employees often meet the following criteria.

- ▶ *They are loners.* To quote one security manager: "Birds of a feather flock together. But bad eggs usually keep to themselves."

- ▶ *If they are not loners, they stay in a very tight, very private and very controlling clique.* Many thieves work together to create their own Fraud Squad. Perhaps one employee creates a distraction while another steals. One employee may process paperwork that covers the actions of another. If you find employee peer groups that essentially refuse to admit newcomers (that is, possible informants), what you may have is a corps of crooks.

- ▶ *They are very territorial.* Employees who keep you away from their cash registers, their lockers, or their workstations may have a history of theft.

Scenario: The accounts payable clerk is very territorial of his computer or the billing statements. He may be sending bogus bills to the company and using the pilfered proceeds to pay his own bills.

How do you spot an accounts payable clerk who's paying himself off? There are a few good warning signs. Consider the case of the accounts payable clerk who's using his position for corrupt purposes.

Cory is always willing to go to the post office, even though the company doesn't reimburse him for mileage (while he's there he picks up his ill-gotten gains from his post office box). He always seems to have extra money a few days after the company pays its bills (even though paychecks don't coincide with the accounts payable cycle). He has a post office box (and extra checks to deposit—ones that look like the company's) for no apparent reason. He tends to make lunch-time trips to the post office or bank immediately after the payment cycle. He doesn't want anyone to handle the accounts payable checks or envelopes because they might notice the bogus bill. (**Note:** His "company" won't be listed in the telephone book.) In short, the company is losing because Cory wants additional money.

SIGN #3 (continued)

Scenario: Shannon, a retail clerk, won't let other people behind her cash register. That's because they would quickly find out what's behind Shannon's relatively high standard of living.

She has a large bag of the company's small (but expensive) items hidden underneath her counter. When one of Shannon's accomplices, Joe or Micki, comes to her counter she secretly stashes some of her hidden horde into their paid-for parcels.

When people act like they have something to hide, they may indeed be hiding something.

People who keep apart from some or most of their fellow employees may be doing so because they are taking part in unsavory activities. It would be wise to watch them carefully.

Again, why? Because it's your job. Because it's the right thing to do. Because if they're stealing from the company, they're stealing from *you*.

Questions for Consideration

1. Describe a situation that you have observed or know about that is similar to those described in this section:

   _____

   _____

   _____

2. How would you react if you saw a coworker engaged in one of the activities described? Why?

   _____

   _____

   _____

SIGN #4: The Obvious Work Quirk

Many times, employees who steal give themselves away. Something about their work record or work habits will be unusual.

Some of these quirks are obvious. For example, a thief might:

✔ Process a Higher Than Average Number of No Sales

Scenario: A customer purchases a $5 item, tosses a $5 bill on the counter and zips out the door. Instead of ringing up the sale, Kim, the cashier, hits the "no sale" key and pockets the money. If Kim does this often, her higher-than-average "no sale" count should have to be accounted for.

Of course, there are legitimate reasons for no sales. A cashier may hit the "no sale" key to make change for a customer or by mistake. The cashier may accidentally give a customer the wrong change and have to hit the "no sale" key so that she can get back into the till.

✔ Processes Nonexistant Refunds

Scenario: While nobody is looking, Dale, a customer service clerk, processes a $50 cash refund for a toy trumpet. However, there was no customer, no return, no reason for Dale to process the transaction. Except, of course, that he plans on stealing the $50.

Beware the coworker who insists that you handle the refunds, no sales, returns, etc. This employee may be trying to lower his sales numbers to compensate for illegitimate actions.

Employees like Kim and Dale could be caught by exception reports, shoppers and honest employees. Exception reports are generated by computer systems that detect employees who process an unusually high level of no sales, refunds or returns. Dale's employer, seeing his higher-than-average returns, will know not to have too much faith in Dale. Eventually Dale will be caught.

SIGN #4 (continued)

When a company knows that an employee is stealing, it may test that employee with a "shopper." Knowing that Kim is a "no sale" specialist, a shopper could be hired to visit Kim's checkout counter and give her a clear opportunity to steal (for example by buying an even dollar item, putting the exact change on the counter and leaving before Kim can ring up the sale and offer a receipt). Since Kim will have no reason to suspect the shopper, she might take the bait.

You don't want to work with thieves, so when you find somebody abusing the system, let your employer know. A store might eventually catch the crooks with exception reports and shoppers, but these tactics may not identify a bad seed as quickly as you do.

A thief seldom does any of the following:

✔ Checks for Items Under Carts

Scenario: Several shopping carts sail through the checkout counter of Sean, a cashier. Sean "forgets" to check the basket bottoms, so unpurchased items go out the door undetected.

✔ Calls for Price Checks

Scenario: Pat, a sales associate, doesn't call for price checks because he doesn't need them. When his friends come in to "purchase" products, he doesn't ring up most of their items. So what does he need with price checks?

✔ Checks for Smaller Items Hidden Within Larger Ones

Scenario: Stacy never checks her customer's purchases for peculiarities. That's because her friends hide small (usually expensive) items inside larger ones.

A thief will often:

✔ Maintain Steady Sales but Drop Total Sales Revenues

One way a thief works is to take a little off the top from every sale. For example:

Scenarios:
- Austin's customer purchases 10 items at $1 each. The customer gives him a $10 bill. After the customer leaves the store, Austin voids five of the $1 sales and pockets the $5 difference.

- Austin's customer gives him $5 cash for a $5 item and, without waiting for a receipt, leaves. Austin rings up the sale for $2.50. He keeps the "change."

- Austin's customer gives him $10 to pay for 10 $1 items. She doesn't look at the receipt, which shows that she purchased eight $1 items.

- Austin is supposed to ring up two items at $2 apiece. He rings up the items at $1.50 each. The customer hands him $4. Austin keeps the $1.

✔ Has Unusually High Absenteeism Rate or Unusual Amounts of Travel

Scenario: Toby always seems to be on the road. He is often late for work and sometimes he does not show up at all. Last week you noticed his car had a new set of tires—again! This is his second set in ten months.

Fencing stolen goods and hiding large amounts of cash aren't easy. For some thieves, it's almost a second career—a time-consuming one that takes them away from work and away from home.

✔ Looks Too Good to Be True

Scenario: Jake is always at work before you get there. And usually he is there after you leave. Twice on weekends you stopped by work to pick up papers you forgot and Jake was there. You are beginning to wonder if Jake ever goes home.

If an employee is the first to arrive and the last to leave (without reason) or has repeated, unusual or unaccompanied overtime, it could be because an employee who is on the premises alone has the perfect opportunity to steal.

If something looks too good (or too unusual) to be true, it probably is. Employees whose performance or work records fall outside the norm may be dishonest.

SIGN #4 (continued)

Questions for Consideration

1. Describe a situation in your workplace similar to those described.

   _____

   _____

   _____

2. What behaviors specifically made you suspicious?

   _____

   _____

   _____

3. If you heard rumors about impending layoffs at your organization because of poor profits, how differently would you act about letting management know that a peer was stealing?

   _____

   _____

   _____

SIGN #5: The Cautious Crook

Did you ever work with someone who asked countless questions or tried to gain information or access that wasn't necessary? If you thought your coworker was bucking for a promotion, think again. He or she may have been analyzing ways to steal from your company.

Scenario: I have been working as a pizza delivery driver for the past two and a half years. *Although I consider myself an honest person, I must admit I have stolen money and products from the company on several occasions.**

The night I began work was also the night the store opened. Both the drivers and managers were inexperienced in the operation of the store, so no one really had a grasp on what to do, especially the managers.

The operation ran on a kind of honor system. The manager gave me a bank of cash to make change. At the end of the night, I gave back the bank plus the total for all the deliveries I had made.

I kept records of my deliveries and the total I collected—the manager took it on faith that I would keep an accurate record. No one checked on my bookkeeping.

After the first few months of my employment, I realized I could get away with stealing by taking the order tickets. But I didn't, because I felt stealing was wrong.

Some of my friends got the same idea, started to steal and didn't get caught. I was upset, because I always believed that if you stole, you would get caught. I assumed that even if the store's manager didn't catch you stealing, then the company's central office or auditors would discover a pizza ticket missing. I wasn't convinced that I could get away with it, but after several months I asked around.

I approached the managers to see if missing tickets could be caught on their paperwork. There was a way, but the managers didn't use it. They received computer counts of the total number of pizza tickets from the main ordering center. They could have subtracted the number of tickets they had received from drivers and the number of cancellations from this number to find out if any order tickets were missing.

SIGN #5 (continued)

One night, when I worked the closing shift with the assistant manager, we had about 350 orders. A check of the paperwork revealed a discrepancy of about 10 tickets. When I asked him about this, he shrugged his shoulders and said he didn't care. He said all he was worried about was having the right amount of money and not coming up short. When I asked how he knew how much money he was supposed to have, he said he tallied the record logs of all the delivery drivers. When asked if he had any independent record other than the delivery drivers' log sheets, he said there was none and asked why I thought there needed to be one.

Now I was positive I wouldn't get caught. My friend's experiences proved that, and I could definitely use the money. On the other hand, the manager could finally see this obvious way to steal and catch me. I thought that I could not risk the possibility of getting caught. It would not only embarrass me, but it would embarrass my family if they knew. I didn't want to risk having to tell my parents that I was fired, or worse yet, that I was being tried on embezzlement charges. This major fear kept me from stealing for a while.

Then one night my tips were lousy. I was in a bad mood because I was broke and had hoped to make a lot of money so I could go out of town the next weekend. *I took a delivery to a customer, and he asked if he could keep the ticket as a receipt.*** I agreed and gave it to him. Now I had no record of the pizza I had just delivered. Normally in this situation I would tell the manager what had happened when I returned to the store. He would have a duplicate sent by teletype and give it to me for my log. This time I didn't say a word and didn't record it in my log.

I felt guilty but tried to rationalize my stealing, which turned out to be easy. First, all my friends were stealing, so I was not alone. My best friend was also working as a driver and we would joke about how much we had taken on a particular night. I even boasted to him that one night I "misplaced" a $70 order.

I also told myself that, since the store grossed about $15,000 a week, they could afford it. *They were charging an outrageous amount for the product and making a killing in profit, or so I thought.****

* Notice the inconsistency: I steal but I'm an honest person.

** This technique is often used by honesty shoppers to catch dishonest employees.

*** Prices are raised when internal costs go up.

Questions for Consideration

1. Why was this employee's lack of tips or the store's seemingly high sales volume not a valid justification for stealing from his employer?

_____

_____

_____

2. If you were the owner of this establishment, what errors or omissions in operations would you fix?

_____

_____

_____

3. Identify the "losers" in this scenario and what each loses.

_____

_____

_____

44

SIGN #6: Unrealistic Reactions

Scenario #1: Lou wins a $100 million lottery. "Big deal," he mutters in disgust. "Probably most of it will go for taxes anyway."

Scenario #2: Jackie sees a three-carat diamond just lying in the gutter. She brushes it off, takes a good look and throws it back into the ditch. "Not big enough," she sighs as she saunters away.

Scenario #3: Brook, a $9-an-hour drink-department assistant manager who is in charge of inventory, is promoted to Head Waterboy in charge of overall department profits. His new position pays more than $12 an hour, but Brook fights tooth and nail to continue his clerk work.

Odds are, scenario #1 or #2 won't happen, but scenario #3—odd as it is—is a common occurrence. Why? Because Brook steals.

How? Brook is an inventory padder, both on the up- and downside. Here's how he does it.

✔ Brook Manipulates Merchandise Value

Scenario: Brook receives merchandise worth $500 retail. He reports its retail value at $400, but the merchandise is sold for the full $500. Thanks to a little financial finagling, Brook can pocket the $100 difference.

✔ Brook Manipulates Merchandise Markdowns

Scenario: The store has 200 bottles of Designer Water in stock, which usually retail for $2 per bottle. The main office directs Brook to sell his remaining merchandise for $1 a bottle.

Brook informs the main office that he has 300 bottles of the bubbly out back. The *true* value of his inventory has been reduced by $200 (200 bottles each reduced by $1). However, *on paper* Brook shows a value reduction of $300 (200 true bottles each reduced by $1 plus 100 mythical bottles each reduced by $1). With a little creative bookkeeping, Brook will be able to pocket the $100 discrepancy.

Brook's employer won't see the missing funds because the books balance.

	The Real Truth	The "Truth" According to Brook
Bottles on hand	200	300
Current inventory value	$200	$300
Product sells for	$200	$200
Brook steals		$100
Discrepancy between value/sales	$0	
Discrepancy between value/sales-theft		$0

See? No problem!

✔ Brook Manipulates Merchandise Markups

Scenario: Brook has 200 bottles of wine cooler in stock. Retailing for $1 a bottle, it has an inventory value of $200.

The main office calls and informs Brook that the retail price of the cooler is going up. The price per bottle is now $1.50.

Brook informs the main office that he has only 100 bottles of the popular coolers. In truth, he has 200.

The true value of Brook's inventory has been increased by $100 (200 bottles each increased $0.50 in value). However, *on paper* Brook shows a value increase of only $50 (100 bottles each increased in value by $0.50). Assuming that all 200 bottles will sell for the designated $1.50 with a little more creative bookkeeping Brook will be able to pocket another $150 in "discrepancies" ($150 in "paper" inventory plus $150 in theft equals the $300 in cooler revenues).

SIGN #6 (continued)

Again, Brook's employer won't see the missing funds because the books balance.

	The Real Truth	The "Truth" According to Brook
Bottles on hand	200	100
Current inventory value	$300	$150
Product sells for	$300	$300
Brook steals		$150
Discrepancy between value/sales	$0	
Discrepancy between value-theft/sales		$0

It's no wonder Brook doesn't want to move on—he's currently moving a lot of the company's money (tax free!) into his own pocket.

It's worth remembering: Those who turn down what look like a good deal, may do so because they don't want to turn their backs on an even better one.

Questions for Consideration

1. Have you worked with someone who you believe padded or manipulated inventory or merchandise values?

   _____

   _____

   _____

2. What did this person do that made you suspicious?

   _____

   _____

   _____

3. List tangible and intangible damage to a company done by an employee like this.

   _____

   _____

SIGN #7: Meaningful Moves

Most of the first six of the Seven Signs are basically warning signs. The following clues, however, tend to have a greater importance. Spot these sure-fire clues and you can be 99% sure that your company is getting burned. Watch for:

✔ Employees Who Keep Unusual Amounts of Merchandise/ Supplies Around Their Work Area

Scenario: Francis, an accounting clerk, keeps a pile of mechanical pencils, expensive fine point pens and calculator paper by his side. He has enough extra envelopes, stamps, ink pads and computer disks at his desk to start his own business supply store. In fact, Francis has been stealing these items for months. Some he keeps, some he sells.

There's nothing wrong with keeping extra supplies at a workstation, but when an employee stores extra items with the determination of a squirrel hoarding nuts, it might mean the company can expect shortages. Find a hoarder and you might have found a theif.

✔ Employees Who Keep Lists of Numbers, a Personal Calculator or Coins in Strange Places

Scenario: Bea, a cashier, keeps piles of pennies in her work smock. Whenever she shorts the company by $1 (through a phony refund, void, no sale or return) she puts a penny by the back corner of her register. At the end of the day, if she has collected 10 pennies, she takes $10 from the till.

Scenario: Dee and Frank don't want to limit themselves to even-dollar deceits. They keep track of their thefts with a calculator or a sheet of paper. At the end of the day, they take their calculated total out of the till.

If you find noncommission employees carefully tracking their sales, beware! They may be tracking their ill-gotten gains.

✔ Employees Who Park Their Cars, or Themselves, in High-Theft Areas

Scenario: Chris, a shipping dock staffer, always parks as close as possible to the shipping docks. By doing so he makes it easier, and less risky, to move the merchandise he steals from store to car door.

Scenario: Les works in the gardening department of a major mass merchandiser. However, he hangs out however in the jewelry department. It's possible that Les is more interested in rocks than in roses, but he might be interested in stealing. It is easier to steal a $25 ring than five pounds of peat moss; furthermore, jewelry is a good gift or easily sold.

Keep an eye on employees who inexplicably spend their time in high-theft areas. Traditionally, these are as follows:

Department	Percentage of theft that this department will account for in a department store
Records, cassettes, CDs, videotapes	5.53
Fashion accessories and costume jewelry	5.41
Radios, television sets, stereos	3.86
Sporting goods	2.95
Juniors' apparel	2.84
Ladies' apparel	2.78
Toys, hobbies, games	2.42
Men's apparel	2.19
Health and beauty aids	1.73
Fine jewelry	1.68
Shoes	1.50

SIGN #7 (continued)

✔ Employees Who "Gain Weight" During the Day

Some employees think of themselves as giant turkeys. They stuff clothing, food, electronics or other merchandise into clothes, purses, parcels or backpacks and fly the coop.

✔ Employees Who Cover Their Cash Register Displays

Scenario: Michael has a sign—"We appreciate your patronage"—taped to the front of his cash register. However, his pleasant sign is really a danger sign.

Let's say Michael receives a $5 bill from a customer who is purchasing a $4.99 item. Michael hits the no-sale key to open the till, hands the customer a penny, and bags the merchandise. The customer doesn't see the "no sale" on Michael's hidden register display, but he does hear the register. He naturally assumes that the sale was properly recorded. Any others in the vicinity (other clerks, other customers, etc.) assume the same.

It's worth remembering: When things are obscured, a theft may have occurred.

✔ Employees Who Have a High Number of "Accidents"

You've already read how restaurant employees broke wine bottles so that their employer would think the beverages were dropped, not drunk. Here are more examples:

Scenario: Carrie, a waitress at an expensive club, regularly spills wine into the cash register. While the machine is down, she can void items on manually written checks or take money without processing sales.

Scenario: Leslie, a stockperson who loves nice clothes, often smears mud on merchandise so that she can buy it for a reduced price.

✔ Employees Who Display All the Wrong Moves

Scenario: Carl, a behind-the-counter clerk, is continually in motion. He turns to the left and right instead of facing the customer, he bobs up and down behind the register. What's going on?

Stolen merchandise is going right out the front door. He looks to make sure nobody is watching. He reaches down to snap up some expensive merchandise he has hidden at his feet. Quick as a wink, he slips it into his accomplice's parcel. His accomplice leaves the store.

Of all the Seven Signs, these clues are most likely to help you realize when someone is stealing.

Questions for Consideration

1. Have you noticed any situations similar to those previously mentioned?

   _____

   _____

   _____

2. If you did notice suspicious activities, what prevented you from going to someone in management with your suspicions?_____

   _____

   _____

3. How did *you* lose by your keeping silent? _____

   _____

   _____

THE FATAL FLAWS CHECKLIST

Use a photocopy of the following checklist to collect data about someone you think is stealing.

Name: _____

I have noticed this behavior on a continuous basis (if the behavior was noted on a specific date or dates, write the dates after the behavior):

☐ Lives beyond the combined family means

☐ Pays cash for large purchases or many purchases

☐ Is a loner

☐ Stays within a tight, private, controlling clique

☐ Is unusually territorial

☐ Has many friends going through his checkout line

☐ Has an unusually high number of no sales

☐ Has an unusually high number of refunds

☐ Has an unusually high number of returns

☐ Asks others to process no sales or refunds

☐ Doesn't check under carts

☐ Doesn't call for price checks

☐ Doesn't check for small items inside larger ones

☐ Maintains a high number of sales but experiences a drop in total sales revenue

☐ Has a high absenteeism rate

☐ Has an inordinately high travel rate

☐ Without reason, is often the first to work or the last to leave

☐ Shows repeated, unusual, unaccompanied overtime

☐ Asks too many questions

☐ Refuses desirable promotions or transfers

☐ Keeps unnecessary merchandise or supplies at work area

☐ Keeps a private list of numbers

☐ Keeps a calculator available (and only for personal use)

☐ Keeps coins in strange places

☐ Parks in high-theft areas

☐ Inexplicably hangs around high-theft areas

☐ "Gains weight" during the day

☐ Covers cash register display

☐ Has a high accident rate

☐ Makes unusual physical moves (inexplicably moves very quickly, up and down, left and right)

This form may be reproduced without further permission from the publisher.

SUMMARY

Catching crooked colleagues isn't difficult. It's just a matter of being alert.

Keep the Seven Signs in mind.

- ► Employees who maintain behaviors, lifestyles, financial obligations and addictions they couldn't possibly afford on their family income

- ► Employees who are socially out of sync with most of their colleagues

- ► Employees whose work records conflict with transaction types, sales, absenteeism, travel or overtime

- ► Employees who ask too many questions

- ► Employees who have a strong negative reaction to positive or neutral news

- ► Employees who perform strange rituals (using pennies or calculators to keep track of thefts, keep too much inventory near their work place, camouflage their cash registers, etc.)

Perhaps most important: Remember that the first sign is one committed by honest employees—deciding that a colleague is honest or dishonest based strictly on surface clues. People are innocent until proven guilty, and you shouldn't decide they're guilty.

PART

IV

Do the Right Thing

MAKING THE DECISION

Doing the right thing doesn't mean it's the easy thing to do.

Helping your employer catch a crooked colleague can put you in a tough position. You don't want to condone theft, but you don't want to condemn your friends, either. You don't want to "snitch," but you don't want thieves to get away with stealing.

Well, not to worry. As you'll see from the following monologues (collected by Northwest Security Managers), most employees feel good after they "do good." You can't blame yourself for doing the right—and sometimes the hard—thing.

CASE #1: Stealing Is Stealing

Once I knew for sure that Forrest was stealing from the company, I knew what I had to do. I kept close track of what Forrest did and as soon as I had a strong case, I took it to our operations manager. From then on it was out of my hands. The security manager handled the whole investigation. I didn't even have to testify at Forrest's trial.

I don't know why anybody would think twice about turning in someone who steals. The way I look at it, if Forrest had stolen a little old lady's purse, I would have turned him in. If I'd seen Forrest steal money from another employee's wallet, I would have turned him in. Stealing from the company isn't any different. Stealing is just plain wrong. It doesn't matter whom you're stealing from.

If you don't turn in a thief just because the victim was a company, then you're blaming the victim for the crime. That's just not fair.

The company didn't make Forrest steal. He made that decision himself, and he has to live with the consequences.

MAKING THE DECISION (continued)

CASE #2: Profit "Taking"

I guess I knew that Marta was stealing stuff from the company, but I didn't want to turn her in because she was my friend. Plus I thought that if anybody found out what I had done, they wouldn't want me around.

Besides, Marta didn't steal all that much. Maybe five or ten dollars' worth of stuff a day. It just didn't seem like that big a deal.

I realized I was wrong when we got our first profit sharing information. The company had suggested not giving us raises last year and, instead, giving us profit sharing. We were sure the company was dividing a big pie, so we agreed.

Boy, was I surprised when I saw the numbers! The company didn't make nearly as much money as I thought it did. But what was really shocking was the stock shortages. Merchandise shortages was one of our biggest expenses. Stealing cost more than our utilities!

That was when I realized that even small thefts could add up to big bucks. I was mad thinking about how Marta's stealing had taken money out of my bonus package. She was rewarded for stealing and I was being penalized for being honest. No more. I secretly told the manager what Marta was doing and it didn't take him long to catch her. Nobody knew what I had done, but I wouldn't have cared if they did. I did the right thing, even though I waited a long time to do it.

CASE #3: Under A Microscope

I didn't mind reporting Greg to the company because I could do it anonymously and not take any flack.

I did it for a couple of reasons. First, I was tired of watching Greg steal and his making excuses about how the company "owed him." We weren't paid very much, but we knew we weren't going to get rich when we took the job.

Second, I got tired of the managers always hanging over us like vultures. I felt like a bug under a microscope. I wasn't doing anything wrong, and I resented the implication that I was. The only way to stop managers from breathing down our necks was to get rid of the theft problem. That meant getting rid of Greg.

Third, I figured that if Greg had decided to steal, he was prepared to get caught. I mean, eventually with or without my help the company would have caught him. The boss was pretty open about the anti-theft procedures. Greg took the gamble and he lost.

I didn't turn Greg in for the reward. The money was a surprise. It's like when you find somebody's wallet and they give you a reward. You don't give the wallet back to them for the reward, but it's nice to know that they appreciate what you've done.

MAKING THE DECISION (continued)

CASE #4: Mom Was Right

I know it sounds silly, but the reason I turned Sasha in was my mother.

I saw Sasha steal money almost every day, maybe $10 or $15, and I knew that I should tell the manager. Stealing is wrong. Still, I didn't want people to think I was a snitch. I worried a lot about what I should do.

Then I thought about what my mother would say. She would have told me that I had two choices: I could report the theft and do what I knew was the right thing; or I could keep quiet about it, which meant I was a part of the theft. If I did the first thing, she would be proud of me and, of course, I could be proud of myself. If I did the second, she would be very disappointed in me. Eventually, so would I.

Well, I turned in Sasha and I did feel good about it. I don't care if anybody else hears about it. I won't be ashamed of doing the right thing.

CASE #5: Feelings

You might think it was hard deciding whether or not to report Bea in for stealing, but it wasn't hard at all.

You see, the decision wasn't about Bea. She was definitely stealing. That was a fact.

The decision was about *me*: how I'd feel about myself if I turned her in, how I'd feel about myself if I didn't. I didn't want to be an accomplice to a thief. I wanted to feel good about myself. Being involved in a theft wouldn't have been the way.

CASE #6: A Win/Win Situation

I turned Terry in because he was selling our construction supplies and using the money to buy himself drugs. We work with a lot of heavy equipment here, and a person who's not in control can do a lot of damage. He could kill himself or somebody else.

I hang with a lot of guys who aren't exactly pro-management, but I was more worried about my skin than about what anybody else would think. As it turned out, the others on my crew were glad I turned Terry in because they were also worried about his using drugs. They knew he could slip up and hurt somebody.

It turned out pretty good for everybody. The company didn't press charges against Terry. Instead, they got him into a drug rehabilitation program and he's doing OK. He'll also have to pay them back for the stuff he stole. So I guess telling the boss about Terry was the best thing I could have done.

TIPS FOR TURNING IN

Some employees choose to address their coworkers rather than their employers. They let their colleagues know that those who steal will eventually be caught or turned in. If that stops the thefts, great. If it doesn't, it's less difficult to turn in a coworker than you might think. Consider this: It's not your job to document fully any crime you suspect. Simply let your managers know if you think there is reason for concern. You can do this in a variety of ways.

- Through your company's formal theft reporting system (if it has one)

- Through an anonymous* phone call

- Through an anonymous* letter

- Through an anonymous* phone message left with the after hours service or on the answering machine

- By filling out a copy of the Seven Signs checklist against your colleague and giving it to your employer

- Discussing your coworker's behavior with your employer

---

*To protect themselves from from the legal implications of slander, managers will conduct confidential investigations of any accusations, whether or not they are anonymous.

NOW IT'S UP TO YOU

According to the National Retail Security Federation, tips from coworkers account for 40% of all detected employee pilfering.

Your company needs you. Your company needs you to do the right thing. To do the smart thing. To do your job. To help stop crime.

It needs you to be aware that internal theft is a major corporate problem—$120 billion a year in employee theft is nothing to sneeze at. It means that employers have to spend a lot of money that could have been used in more productive and beneficial ways.

Your company needs you to recognize that employee theft hurts everybody. Money spent to cover shortages can't be spent on bigger raises, bonuses, profit sharing, retirement contributions or benefits. Internal theft creates an "us vs. them" mentality. It flaunts unfairness. Internal theft also makes it more difficult for the honest employees to do their jobs.

Your company needs you to be aware of the Seven Signs, the clues that indicate that someone might be pilfering. Just as a theft-free environment leads to a more pleasant and profitable job, a knowledge of the Seven Signs can lead to more easily recognized theft.

Your company needs you to realize that turning in pilfering employees is the right thing to do. Not the easy thing: the *right* thing.

NOTES

NOTES

NOTES

NOTES

NOTES

NOTES

OVER 150 BOOKS AND 35 VIDEOS AVAILABLE IN THE 50-MINUTE SERIES

We hope you enjoyed this book. If so, we have good news for you. This title is part of the best-selling *50-MINUTE™ Series* of books. All *Series* books are similar in size and identical in price. Many are supported with training videos.

To order *50-MINUTE* Books and Videos or request a free catalog, contact your local distributor or Crisp Publications, Inc., 1200 Hamilton Court, Menlo Park, CA 94025. Our toll-free number is (800) 442-7477.

50-Minute Series Books and Videos Subject Areas . . .

Management
Training
Human Resources
Customer Service and Sales Training
Communications
Small Business and Financial Planning
Creativity
Personal Development
Wellness
Adult Literacy and Learning
Career, Retirement and Life Planning

Other titles available from Crisp Publications in these categories

Crisp Computer Series
The Crisp Small Business & Entrepreneurship Series
Quick Read Series
Management
Personal Development
Retirement Planning